CAT vs HUMAN

FAIRY TAILS

CAT vs HUMAN

FAIRY TAILS

YASMINE SUROVEC

Andrews McMeel
Publishing®

a division of Andrews McMeel Universal

Contents

EVERY TIME RAPUNZEL WOULD LET HER HAIR DOWN,

SHE WOULD GAIN MORE FRIENDS.

4

5

GOLDILOCKS

ONCE THERE WAS A TIRED AND SLEEPY KITTY...

WHO CHANCED UPON A LITTLE COTTAGE.

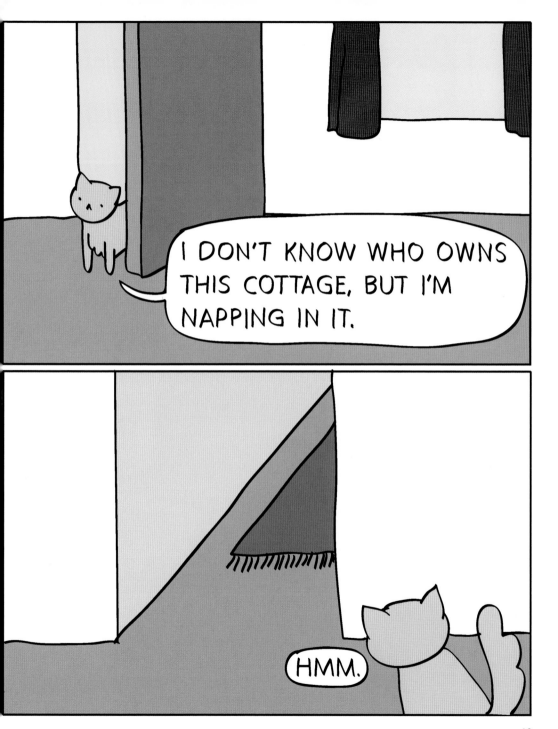

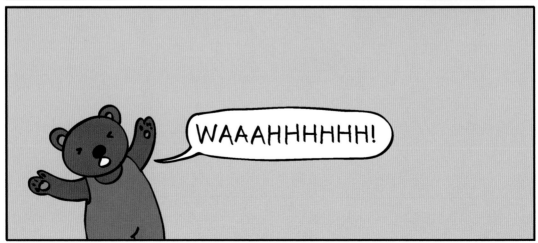

THE UGLY KITTEN

THE PRINCESS AND THE KITTY

THE PRINCE AND PRINCESS SOON MARRY.
AND WE LIVED HAPPILY EVER AFTER!

44

And they lived happily ever after.

THE PRINCESS AND THE PEA

RUMBLE!

?!

I WONDER WHAT'S IN HERE.

EEP!

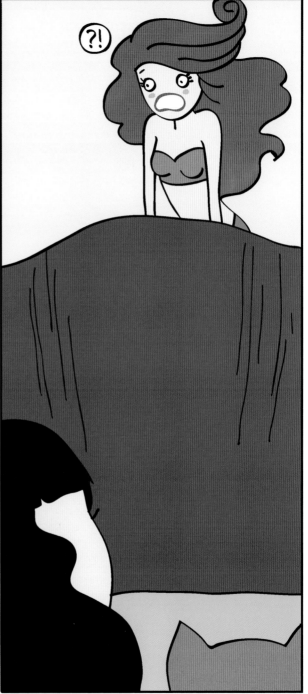

SLEEPING BEAUTY

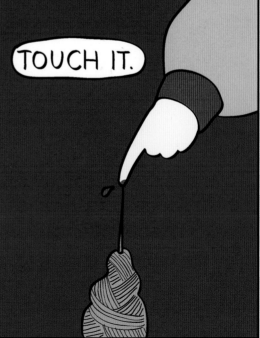

AND THE LONELY GRAY KITTY FOUND HIS FOREVER HOME.

I'M SO COLD.

SIGH.

PURR

MMM...WARM AND FLUFFY!

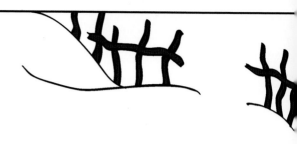

ALSO BY YASMINE SUROVEC:

YASMINE SUROVEC IS
AN ILLUSTRATOR AND
CARTOONIST WHO DIVIDES
HER TIME BETWEEN
CALIFORNIA AND ARIZONA
WITH HER HUSBAND, THREE
KITTIES, AND PUPPY.

Andrews McMeel Publishing
a division of Andrews McMeel Universal
1130 Walnut Street, Kansas City, Missouri 64106

www.andrewsmcmeel.com

16 17 18 19 20 SDB 10 9 8 7 6 5 4 3 2 1

ISBN: 978-1-4494-7068-5

Library of Congress Control Number: 2016936010

Editor: Patty Rice
Art Director/Designer: Diane Marsh
Production Manager: Tamara Haus
Production Editor: Erika Kuster

ATTENTION: SCHOOLS AND BUSINESSES
Andrews McMeel books are available at quantity discounts with bulk purchase for educational, business, or sales promotional use. For information, please e-mail the Andrews McMeel Publishing Special Sales Department: specialsales@amuniversal.com.

Why not use Allan Pease as guest speaker for your next conference or seminar?

Pease International (Australia) Pty Ltd
Pease International (UK) Ltd

P.O. Box 1260
Buderim 4556
Queensland
AUSTRALIA
Tel: ++61 7 5445 5600
Fax: ++61 7 5445 5688

Liberty House
16 Newbold Terrace
Leamington Spa CV 32 4 EG
UNITED KINGDOM
Tel: ++44 (0) 1926 889900
Fax: ++44 (0) 1926 421100

email: (Aust) info@peaseinternational.com
            (UK) ukoffice@peaseinternational.com
website: www.peaseinternational.com

Also by Allan Pease:

Video Programs
Body Language Series
Silent Signals
The Interview
How to Make Appointments by Telephone

DVD Programs
The Best of Body Language
How to Develop Powerful Communication—Managing the Differences Between Men and Women

Audio Programs
The Four Personality Styles
How to Make Appointments by Telephone
How to Remember Names, Faces & Lists
Why Men Don't Listen and Women Can't Read Maps
Questions are the Answers

Books
The Definitive Book of Body Language
Why Men Don't Listen & Women Can't Read Maps
Why Men Don't Have a Clue and Women Always Need More Shoes
Why Men Can Only Do One Thing At A Time & Women Never Stop Talking
How Compatible Are You?
Talk Language
Write Language
Questions are the Answers
The Bumper Book of Rude & Politically Incorrect Jokes
Politically Incorrect Jokes Men Love

By Allan and Barbara Pease

THE DEFINITIVE BOOK OF BODY LANGUAGE

WHY MEN DON'T HAVE A CLUE AND
WOMEN ALWAYS NEED MORE SHOES

WHY MEN DON'T LISTEN AND
WOMEN CAN'T READ MAPS

QUESTIONS ARE THE ANSWERS

TALK LANGUAGE

WHY MEN CAN ONLY DO ONE THING AT A TIME
AND WOMEN NEVER STOP TALKING